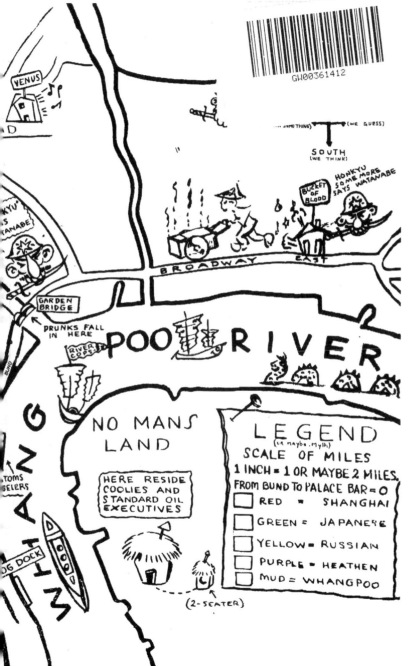

SHANGHAI
HIGH LIGHTS
LOW LIGHTS
TAEL LIGHTS

SHANGHAI
HIGH LIGHTS
LOW LIGHTS
TAEL LIGHTS

by Maurine Karns & Pat Patterson

With a New Foreword by Michael Schoenhals

First Published in 1936
Reprinted by Earnshaw Books
Hong Kong 2009

EARNSHAW
BOOKS

Shanghai: High Lights, Low Lights, Tael Lights

By Maurine Karns & Pat Patterson

With a foreword by Michael Schoenhals

ISBN-13: 978-988-17621-0-8

Shanghai: High Lights, Low Lights, Tael Lights was first published in 1936.
This edition with a new foreword is reprinted by
China Economic Review Publishing (HK) Limited for Earnshaw Books
1804, 18/F New Victory House,
93-103 Wing Lok Street, Sheung Wan, Hong Kong

Series Editor: Andrew Chubb

This book has been reset in 12pt Book Antiqua. Spellings and punctuations are left as in the original edition.

IN MEMORY OF PAT PATTERSON

This book, a light-hearted introduction to the seamier side of Shanghai, dates from the mid-1930s. I knew the co-author Pat Patterson in Hong Kong in the mid-1970s. He was an extraordinary man, a Canadian with a vast appetite for everything life and Asia had to offer. He was a pilot, and represented all the major U.S. aircraft manufacturers in China in the 1930s. He held the second of only two private pilot licenses ever issued in China, and once told me that he sky-wrote the character for long life in the skies above Shanghai in honor of Madame Chiang Kai-shek. He was a man of legend in the bars of Hong Kong, but his drinking partners were mostly unaware of Pat's excursion into the literary world.

Please do not write in to tell us that there are mistakes in some of the spelling and grammar. We know. This is how the authors wrote it, probably in a whangpoo whiskey haze, and who are we to correct them? The book remains as it was, warts (only a few) and all.

Graham Earnshaw
Publisher

Foreword

By Michael Schoenhals

I FIRST STUMBLED across *Shanghai: High Lights Low Lights Tael Lights* in the Fudan University library in the winter of 1975. I had arrived in the big city in October, by train from Beijing. The harsh, dirty, early 20th century industrialized city skyline reminded me of Omaha, Nebraska, though the water tasted different.

There were only a dozen foreign students from capitalist countries in Shanghai at that time, a year before Chairman Mao died. We led a privileged existence: our dorm rooms had heating and only triple occupancy. I was twenty-two years old, listened on a shortwave radio by night to Willis Conover jazz shows on the Voice of America and poured in silence over Nietzsche, while my two Chinese roommates sought to divine the future of the revolution and their place in it by reading between the lines of the People's Daily.

For some reason, the Fudan University library kept a lot of "poisonous weeds" in the reading room, trashy feudal and revisionist novels with little slips of paper glued to the inside cover inviting students to present a denunciation of the work in question at the front desk before leaving. There was also a card catalogue which listed titles in foreign languages, books kept somewhere in the back but available on demand. It was to these old books on Shanghai that my interest soon turned: to the books that described a different, exciting, wild place.

Shanghai in the ninth year of the Cultural Revolution was unbelievably boring most of the time. Okay, so a tram ride to Hongkew Park was fun . . . sort of. And the burgers on offer at the Cosmo, the only remaining Western eatery in city central, were superb. The waiters, speaking in pidgin English of the 1949 communist victory, referred not to "Liberation" but to "when bossman go home".

For ten whole days, as part of our

education, we foreign students even got
to work in a Yangtszepoo factory — to not
just mingle but to work with the industrial
proletariat. But most of the time, Shanghai
was dull. What better way of getting away
from it while also remaining in place than
to self-immerse in 1930s guidebooks and
then move around on bicycle in search of old
Shanghai?

Of all my extracurricular reading that
year, none left a deeper impression than
Shanghai: High Lights, Low Lights, Tael Lights.
I had never seen or heard of anything like it
before. Had I been asked, I would have said
that no such book could possibly exist; and
if — let's assume, just for the sake of it — such
a book had once existed, then surely, the
Cultural Revolution with all its supposedly
systematic "destruction of the four olds"
would have (a) threat-listed, (b) liberated,
and (c) pulped it — not simply left it in the
library of our university. (A university which,
incidentally, the 1974 "For Official Use Only"
*Brief Introductions to Units in Open Cities and
Regions that May be Visited* [by foreigners]

described as setting an excellent example for other revolutionary institutions of higher learning to follow). But there it was.

The original hand-drawn map left the old Chinese city blank, and the accompanying legend consisted of no more than three little words . . . not "I love you," but "Smells originate here!" One chapter (the last one) bore the title, 'There are also some Chinese in Shanghai.' It began: "To most people there are but two kinds of Chinese, the clean and the dirty. However, the situation is more complex than that." I had grown up in the moral superpower of Sweden and lived a sheltered life. I was politically correct and disliked Abba intensely. My initial reaction was: "You can say that? And get away with it?"

Strangely attractive about Karns and Patterson was, I discovered, that they had expertise (which I myself desired) and chutzpa (of which I had none). They announced they were "pioneers of a New Group" of people writing about Shanghai, those who "know very little about it, but

know a hell of a lot about that very little."
By 1975, however, there was little left of
"that very little". The names dropped in their
chapter on "making whoopee in Shanghai"
were all history: the Tower, the Sky Terrace,
the Paramount Ballroom, the Majestic, the
Ambassador, the Casanova ("all Russian
hostesses"), Del Monte's, Santa Anna's on
Love Lane, and the Venus Café in Hongkew.
On one of my urban archaeologist's
bicycle tours I actually managed to locate
possible remnants of the Venus Café: over
a crumbling entrance archway off North
Szechuen Road, the lower right-hand corner
of a billboard that said "Long Live Mao
Zedong Thought" had fallen off, revealing
the letters "ing" in neon lights. I still like to
believe they had spelled the end of the word
"Dancing"!

By comparison to the authors of other
early 20th century guides to Shanghai,
Karns and Patterson are vulgar, informative,
and in your face. A. G. Hickmott's 1921
Guide to Shanghai wasted print on the
Jewish Cemetery, Victoria Nursing Home,

locomotion ("The vehicles of locomotion
used in Shanghai are motor cars, pony
carriages, rickshas and tramcars"), and
distances to other cities (Vancouver: 5,013
miles). Karns and Patterson focused
instead on "How to kill a lonely evening in
Shanghai," "Other Sidewalk Phenonemae,"
and "Nymphs de Pave." Infinitely more
interesting to a visitor, I thought. "Bunk!" —
the owner of an original copy of *Tael Lights*
had penciled in the margin next to where
Karns and Patterson claimed: "The morals of
the class are about the same as respectable
women everywhere, that is adamantly
negative most of the time, charmingly
complaisant upon occasion."

How they came up with their quirky
book title is a mystery. Perhaps they
were inspired by the writer L.Z. Yuan, a
contemporary of theirs, whose daily column
(described by his publisher as "sparkling
and informative paragraphs") in the
Shanghai Evening Post & Mercury was called
'Sidelights on Shanghai.' But where Yuan
wrote, predictably, of the "Paris of the Far

East," Karns and Patterson insisted instead on calling Shanghai a "multi-colored and complex Bagdad-on-the Whangpoo."

Which brings me around to why I believe *Shanghai: High Lights, Low Lights, Tael Lights* deserves to be read by a wider audience and why Graham Earnshaw is showing such foresight by publishing this new edition. In its tactless self-irony, it retroactively foreshadows like no other work the globalized Shanghai of the 21st century — "not an atmospheric background for Oriental melodrama, but a grand place to live, to work and to enjoy life."

Enjoy!

Michael Schoenhals, Professor
Centre for Languages and Literature
Lund University
December 2008

With grateful acknowledgements to

V. Edward Smith, C.N.A.C.

For the contribution of all full page illustrations

Also to Dr. William E. Walsh, M.C., U.S.N. our friendly

Simon Legree

First Edition

April 1936.

COPYRIGHTED

Contents

meet me by the slop chute
   on the old whang-poo
      bring along your dip net
         there'll be enough for two
           there'll be mashed potatoes
         and some irish stew
           meet me by the slop chute
             on the old whang-poo

an explanation
but not an apology

SHANGHAI HAS BEEN written about by
all sorts of people, and in all sorts of veins.
By people who knew all about it, by others
who thought they knew all about it and by
people who knew they didn't know anything
about it but took a chance anyway. We, the
collaborating undersigned, are pioneers of
a New Group. We know very little about it,
but know a hell of a lot about that very little.
At various places throughout this intellectual
treatise, you will find subjects very sketchily
treated. Those are the things we know very
little about. But upon things about which we
are well informed, we have positively spread
ourselves.

The treatment of the subject is also
somewhat of an innovation. Most people
approach the writing of such a work with
either pompous authority, eerie mystery,

or devil-may-care Halliburtonishness. We have done none of these silly things. We have approached it somewhat as a travelling salesman approaches Chicago, with the hope of enjoying ourselves, of making a little money, and of not committing ourselves to anything for which we might be sorry.

Let it be understood that we guarantee absolutely nothing that we say between these covers. The best we can do is suggest that our statements might quite possibly be founded on fact, and we might as well announce that we're prepared for any bad kick-backs. Anything that is proved to be wrong, we intend to blame on Chinese folk-lore.

We have, however, tried to portray the Shanghai scene. Not a minute, detailed, factual panorama of the Whangpoo town. No temples, nor statistics nor dynasty dates. Just a sort of a composite of what Shanghai looks like, and feels like and smells like after, say, the third whiskey-soda, when, as Shakespeare or somebody said, the senses are sharpest.

So here you have our book, for better or for worse.

Who said "so what!"

To the cool appraiser of facts we have nothing to offer. To the person seeking the back-alley eeriness that Hollywood and Sax Rohmer have given Shanghai, we will only come as a wet blanket. To the sociological student seeking start truths about the great hungering masses of Cathay, we will give, happily, a severe headache. But to the person who has laughed at the unconscious absurdity of a cockeyed sign on Foochow Road, or has rubbernecked into a dense knot of Chinese to find a couple of coolies arguing from two ends of a squawking, disgusted chicken, or has burned completely up when the gentleman between the ricsha shafts refuses to do better than a disinterested lope, or has gotten a kick out of the purple dawn across the Race Course from Bubbling Well Road after a night out and around—to such a person, or one who could understand the mood that prompts such activities, we offer this epic volume, this Guide Book to

end Guide Books, this interpretation of a
Shanghai that has somehow failed to get into
tourist books, learned treatises or into the
movies.

MAURINE KARNS,
PAT PATTERSON.

information,
accurate
and
otherwise

the town

QUITE A NUMBER of years ago, somewhat before the Astor House was built, Marco Polo came to China to establish trade routes. He came to the orient with a purpose, accomplished that purpose, and went home again. Marco was apparently the last foreigner coming to China to do all of these things.

Since then Americans and Europeans have been arriving in the Whangpoo City at a rate alarming to the Chinese. Most of them have come without definite purpose, many of them have carried out a purpose formed since their arrival, and most of them were carried away (if away they got) on the same fortuitous tide that brought them to China. Around such a colony the nucleus of the foreign settlement at Shanghai was built. And so there is small wonder that the most unique city in the world has developed here.

Greater Shanghai is divided into three sections, the International Settlement, the French Concession and the Chinese City. The International Settlement is administered by what is euphemistically termed "popular government," that is, a council of fourteen members elected by the various foreign elements living within the Settlement. In view of the large hand that the representative foreign consuls have in assisting the Council in its decisions, it might be said that the state departments, foreign offices and Gaimishus of the countrys involved have as much if not more to say about governing policy in the International Settlement than the residents and voters thereof. Of the fourteen members of the municipal council, there are five British, two Americans, two Japanese —

and — oh yes, five Chinese. The Settlement
has it's own municipal organization, fire
and police departments, etc, not to mention
it's own military organization, the Shanghai
Defense Corps. Members of this organization
wear a very attractive uniform, rehearse their
manouvers frequently out on the country
side and everyone enjoys the work and the
uniforms and marching to the band very
much indeed.

The French Concession is owned
and operated by the French, policed by
the Annamites, lived in by the Russians,
suspected by the Japanese (of being the
center of com-communistic activities), and
visited by Americans in search of a girl
named Tamara, with blond braids, who
dances at St. Georges. The streets have
French names, at least.

The Concession, commonly known as
Frenchtown, is completely under the thumb
of the French Consulate General. Fifty
thousand Frenchmen might be wrong but
the Consul General in Shanghai is apparently
infallible for his decisions are unappealable.

Frenchtown, also, has a municipal council but its council has advisory powers only and France's head man can take or leave their advice and it is rumored about that there is a lot of good advice gathering dust on the Rue de Consulat. In the International Settlement most of the business interests are centered, while a lot of of the monkey business interests are to be found in Frenchtown, especially on Blood Alley, marked on the maps as the Rue Chau Pao San, where there are fifteen cabarets and near-cabarets in the space of one block.

The Chinese City, so called because it is run by the Chinese, is known as Nantao, and will probably be a disappointment as a showplace to anyone outside of an enterprising sanitation engineer. A conscientious guide book says that much has been done to clean up the streets, "although much remains to be done", which is an under-under-statement. With few exceptions there is little to be seen here except native life in the raw, and to many of even the most enthusiastic viewers of native-life-in-the-raw, the going and the smelling in Nantao gets a little rough.

The International Settlement can be subdivided into two sections, the Settlement proper and Hongkew, which is probably the only part of Nationalist China which seems to have recognized "Manchukuo". The principal object of interest in Hongkew, outside of the Venus Café, is the Japanese Landing Party Barracks.

The population of the Settlement itself, outside of Hongkew which is largely inhabited by Japanese so far as foreign populations are concerned, is composed of British and Americans in major quantities and of other nationalities in diminishing amounts. The Britishers outnumber the Americans at the rate of three to one. In Frenchtown, there are almost ten thousand Russians (and it seems like twice that many on a Sunday afternoon on the Avenue Joffre) to about fifteen hundred French.

The bulk of the Russians living in Frenchtown are in extremely indigent circumstances, a large part of them leading virtually a hand-to-mouth existence, with the hand sometimes failing to reach the mouth. Most of them are refugees from the proletarian neighbor in the north, and there mere whispered mention of the Ogpu on the Route Vallon is enough to clear the street.

White Russians in Shanghai are in a pretty tough spot. Without a consul or country to appeal to and without very much class prestige with either the other foreigners or the Chinese, they have a hard time getting on. An abnormally large percentage of their population is unemployed and those who do work receive very poor wages. Many of them compete with the Chinese in the begging business. A large number of Russian girls dance in cabarets making very attractive *woo niuhs*, and hardened by adversity, are well adapted to the business. For the most part, however, Russians in Shanghai have a very tough time of it and yet, withal, make the best of their lot and are on the whole, one of the gayest of foreign groups.

Hongkew, referred to humorously by some as the "Japanese Concession" has

become the dwelling and gat
of Japan's nationals. Nippon
can be viewed quite often playing
late at late at night upon the streets of night
upon the streets of this section. In Hongkew
are also to be found some of the more choice
of Shanghai's night resorts, to be covered in
another section of this treatise.

the main drags

IN TRUE GUIDE book style, we begin at
the Bund, which is the wide avenue which
separates the Whangpoo River from the city.
Along the bund are the stately buildings
which are to be found on the picture post
cards. At the extreme south end of the city's
waterfront is a crummy avenue known as
the French Bund. The Settlement's Bund
commences at the Avenue Edouard VII or
Edward the Seventh Avenue depending on
your sympathies. Going North along this
road, and with your back to the Whangpoo
(if you can negotiate such a feat) you have

rom left to right, a collection something like this, (leaving out those not of interest) the Shanghai Club (longest bar in the world, by gad, suh!), the Hong Kong and Shanghai Bank (with the imposing dome), the Bank of Communications and the Central Bank (two Oriental Big Shots) the Palace and the Cathay Hotels. A few more buildings and just before the ricksha coolie begins to pant at the incline fronting the Garden Bridge, to your left you have the China–side domicile of His Brittanic Majesty, of England, Scotland Ireland and Wales, and points west.

Just on the other side of the Garden Bridge one finds on either side of the road, the Astor House and the sky-scraping Broadway Mansions. Facing the Astor House is the gloomy structure housing the consulate of the Soviet Union. Right next door is Herr Hitler's representative in China. A little further along is the Japanese Consulate. Just one big happy family.

Nanking Road, starting at the Bund and traversing the business part of the Settlement is probably the Town's principle artery. Upon this street are to be found most of the important Chinese and foreign shops, restaurants, etc. Jimmy's and the Chocolate Shop where most foreigners eat and meet, Sun Ya, probably the best spot to get a Chinese dinner, the leading department stores, Wing On, The Sincere Company, The Sun Sun Company, and the newly-built Sun Company – all of these and many more are to be found on Nanking Road.

On Peking Road, running parallel to Nanking Road are furniture stores. Furniture buying is a craft requiring finesse. You step into a shop and choose a piece or order one made. Then inquire about the price. The dealer blandly names a figure way up thar which sounds like the Chinese National debt or the population of Tokyo. Amazed, astounded and slightly hurt you wordlessly leave the premises. A few days later, while accidently passing the place, you drop in to inquire after the welfare of your chosen piece. You find that the price has fallen off somewhat. This goes on for several weeks until the swelling has subsided and the price is nearly normal, or what the dealer wanted in the first place. Then you buy.

Upon reaching Thibet Road, Nanking Road becomes Bubbling Well Road, and as such continues out to the limits of the Settlement. Formerly, Bubbling Well Road was famed for it's beautiful residences but with the encroachments of commerce, the street has become declasse and most of the ritzy dwellings are to be found in Frenchtown.

Paralleling Nanking Road, and emanating from the Bund at the point where the French Concession begins is Avenue Edward VII. This winding street, which used to be a creek, constitutes the boundery between the Settlement and the French Concession. At its termination, it merges into Avenue Foch and this road takes up the responsibility of separating the two communities. Thus, one finds the anomaly of crossing the street from one nation to the other. French traffic police govern the up-flow of traffic, while Settlement police regulate the down flow. At this boundry and

at the northern edge of the settlement are
to be found many cabarets and night spots,
taking advantage of the French and Chinese
permission to remain open for business at
night much later than the more virtuously
governed Settlement spots.

Another important artery, running
westwards from the Bund midway between
Avenue Edward VII and Nanking Road, and
paralleling them, is Foochow Road. Three
blocks above the Bund on Foochow Road,
one leaves the foreign influence behind,
and enters upon a purely Chinese shopping
district. Here are stores, restaurants, hotels
and the town's leading Chinese Theater (at
Yunan Road) catering to Chinese only. Just
beyond the Chinese Theater on Yunnan Road
is the Indian Curry House, probably one of
the best places in Shanghai in which to eat
curry. Below the Race Course and running
transversely from Avenue Edward VII over
to the intersection of Nanking and Bubbling
Well Roads and on over to and across
Soochow Creek (which separates Hongkew
and Chapei from the Settlement proper) is

Thibet Road, upon which many of the large Chinese hotels are located.

Laterally transversing the Settlement and paralleling Thibet Road are Yates Road, sacred to women's clothing shops, Seymour Road, where many foreign boarding and dwelling houses are located, and Avenue Haig, the farthermost western boundry of the settlement.

Shanghai is essentially a small town. Outside of the Japanese, there are not more than thirty or forty thousand foreigners living in the city and only a small percentage of these are English speaking. Thus the town suffers all of the faults, complexities and inhibitions of a small town. Gossip abounds. Everyone's past, present and future prospects are known to most everyone else. And to most of the residents all of the small town taboos are effective. The newspapers are unable to enter the editorially commentative or critical field because of the fact that almost any person, theatrical production, civic condition or what have you that might be subject to editorial comment is protected, closely or remotely, connection with what is spoken of reverently, and with downcast eyes, in Shanghai, as "an advertiser".

the tall building on your right

SHANGHAI LIKE OTHER far-famed places, has it's conventional rubberneck spots, and when the cruise boats are in, the tourists are to be found in large quantities milling around at the Lung Wha Pagoda, fingering their guide books at the Willow Pattern Tea House, and airing their adenoids at the Siccawei Observatory, all grade A tourist stops and sure fire hokum in the repertoire of any professional guide.

As a matter of fact, all of these and others of their type, are a distinct bore. The Lung Wha Pagoda isn't even a very good pagoda, even if you like pagodas, and there are scores of more beautiful pagodas in China. All that one very good guide book can find to say to it's advantage is that "a climb to the top gives an excellent view of the countryside." Well, you can do this at the Park Hotel in an elevator and save the time and expense of a trip to the country. The Willow Pattern Tea House is a rather crummy place in very crummy surroundings. Take our advice and skip it. It is supposed to have been the original of the famous pictured tea house on the willow pattern China ware, but as the china is a good deal older than the tea house is known to be, it can easily be seen that this story is all haywire. And Siccawei Observatory is just another observatory.

In Shanghai itself, we suggest a visit to one of the native Chinese amusement centers, such as the Great World Amusement Company on Thibet Road. This is where the Chinese masses get their entertainment and such places are as typical of Chinese life as Coney Island is of New York. For twenty cents (small money, at that) entrance can be effected into this palace of entertainment. With dozens of stages and booths erected on three floors of the place, and plays, acrobatics, feats of magic, singing and two-headed babies being on view at any and all times of the day and night, it can be easily seen that one gets their money's worth.

Not as large but of equal interest for different reasons is the amusement center on the fifth and sixth floors of the Wing On Department Store on Nanking and Chekiang Roads. To call Wing On's a department store is like calling Barnum and Bailey's an elephant show. In addition to the merchandising departments on the Nanking Road side of the store, there is also, in the same building, a hotel, a large restaurant, a cabaret with more than a hundred dancing girls and twelve-piece orchestra, and the amusement center on the two top floors surmounted with a sort of summer garden on the roof, which is a really excellent place from which to obtain a rather spectacular night view of the mid-town area.

To return to the amusement center, one finds the many stages with gaudily gowned actors doing their stuff, food vendor's booths, even a motion picture theater showing not

very pictorially-coherent Chinese pictures.
However, of most interest are ones fellow
spectators. Blasé, nonchallant indifference to
the whole business characterizes the attitude
of all except the very young. The play goes
on here, but so do the customers, often
getting up and walking on to the next show
in the midst of the climax. Families show
up en masse, bringing with them perhaps
an entire chicken wrapped in cloth, which
they tear limb from limb and noisily gnaw
from the bone, both eyes intently on the play.
Others sit by eating watermelon or sunflower
seeds with sound effects.

Most interesting are the happiness girls,
who crowd to this ideal avenue for their
talents, pursuing the oldest profession (thats
the tip-off) in a manner that would make the
efforts of a boulevard demmondaine seem
effete and ineffectual. Painted and coiffured
to the hilt, they stand about in glassy-eyed
speculation, amahs ever handy. At the peak
of the evening, there are hundreds of them.
Once that they sight on a man who seems to
be a happy compromise of financial affluence

and amorous aptitude, they use everything at their disposal inclusive of their own charm and allure as well as the brawn and perspiration of the amah, to bring him to bay, and usually do. Occasionally, a vainly-wood male will be pursued into the audience seats to the amusement of the other spectators and sometimes the actors and stagehands as well.

Other lovely damsels come to this Oriental Coney Island too. Witness the story of a young man who found himself sitting next to a damsel of much beauty. Painted, scented, powdered to perfection, every hair in place, her gown as colorfully dainty as can be conceived, the young man was quite impressed. He watched her. Presently she took something from her bag and commenced to chew on it. He looked closer. It was a duck's gizzard, dried. Romance took it on the lam.

Anyway, The Wing On Amusement Center is a lot more worth seeing than the Lung Wha Pagoda.

pastimes, pleasures and puerilities

PEOPLE HAVE A good time in Shanghai, often because they have more time in which to enjoy themselves than they would have elsewhere, more often because the number of friends that people have coming through, or staying for a short time gets them into the habit of entertaining and being entertained, but most of all because it is apparently a part of the Shanghai psychology to have as good a time as possible as often as possible. Even the missionaries get around, we understand.

Principle among the methods of diversion seems to be the good old pastime of stepping out. This is done by getting into the glad rags, taking on a few quick ones, going to your favorite evening spot, then somewhere else, and so on, and so on, (see our section on night life) until you wind up at either Del Monte's or the Venus. Then home, bed, milk of magnesia, and late to the office.

Newcomers to Shanghai, upon seeing the magnificent Race Course often got the idea that this forms one of the town's more exciting diversions. Unfortunately, this is not true. Racing in Shanghai is, in the words of our houseboy, no use. The system of betting is, in the first place, all wrong according to the standards of people who enjoy betting horses elsewhere. In the second place, there are no horses in Shanghai — at least, not race horses. There are a number of animals who might possibly get by in the pony class at a Children's Gymkhana elsewhere, but no horses to inspire a bet of five on the nose to win. The horse business, in Shanghai, is in the hands of gentlemen riders, most of whom are at least gentlemen. Some of them ride very well, indeed. A race meet however has the atmosphere of an English fox hunt, and nobody much is interested in an English fox hunt except the hunter and the fox.

Hai Alai, which takes place continuously out in a splendid new auditorium in Frenchtown is interesting, has many followers and is as good a way to lose your shirt as we know of. You can lay a bet here just as easily as you could get converted at the Methodist Mission. Hai Alai is an old Basque game, and the town is filled with Basquards who have been imported to lend the local game an authentic touch.

Dog racing occurs regularly at the Canidrome, also in Frenchtown. Whippets chase each other around the track after a phoney rabbit and a good time is had by all. Betting is on the pari-mutuel system, the club getting fifteen per cent of the take. Betting tickets are bought in two dollar and five dollar denominations. This is as wacky a way to lose your money as we know of.

For those who like to gamble, the State Lottery offers a slower if no surer means to the big money. A ticket costs ten dollars, a share (one tenth part of a ticket) sets you back a dollar. The big prize is 250,000 dollars but there is a complicated system of less important prizes and ones impression upon reading the list of awards is that everyone in China should receive some kind of prize. We have never known anyone who won a pretzel in this lottery, however.

chits, good and otherwise

THE FEMININE WRITER of an extremely entertaining book entitled "Audacious Angles on China" states that "in Shanghai, a person may enter practically any restaurant or cafe and merely inscribe his name and

address on a slip of paper" in settlement
of the account. Either this learned lady
was in Shanghai prior to the depression or
we'd like to get a list of the cabarets and
cafes that she visited for future reference.
In the hallowed past, we are told that this
condition prevailed, and that it was an
unusual thing for a foreigner to carry actual
cash with him. That some personal chits
(China side for IOU) had all of the validity
with persons who knew the signer of the
chit or his reputation, of cash itself, and
that such were passed from hand to hand
like banknotes. This sounds like something
out of Paul Bunyan to us, but be that as it
may, as Aunt Harriet used to say, chits are
off the gold standard today. Many chits are
signed, this is true, and some of them are
even collected, but the Golden Era for the
man who says "Thank God, thats paid!" as
he does an autograph for the table-boy, is
definitely over. Nowadays, cash gets amiable
benevolance, a check gets a wintry smile and
a chit gets Oriental malevolance.

The lady writer goes on to say

(regarding the chit) that they "have no way of checking up on it, nor does he attempt to do so", simply filing it away. Well, our only thought in regard to this is that she should see the wordy research conferences that go on outside while the chit signer is drawing on his gloves and getting ready to go. Corrugated foreheads peer from behind curtains or screens and everyone down to the cigarette boy is included upon an extemporaneously organized Board of Inquiry into the subject's affluence.

Theoretically, the means of collecting these chits is by sending what is commonly known and humorously referred to as a "shroff" to the residence of the chitter in the hope of getting the money. To read from a shroff's report of results sheet, one would gather that the foreign population of Shanghai had suddenly and precipitously departed to escape a second uprising of Boxers. "Out of Town", "Out of Town" with an occasional variation offered by some straight-forward soul in a hopeful "Call around next week." To the average schroff, a payment of about one tenth of the amount involved is victory and is regarded by the debtor as a magnanimous concession. Chits are made of very heavy paper in China these days. They have to stand a lot of wear.

In other countries, the problem is how to get money. The same problem is complicated in China with the additional one of how to count it when you get it. In the first place, there is "'big money" and "small money." All that a foreigner knows about these two species during his first six months in the East is that he is supposed to raise an awful racket when he gets his change in small money. Technically, small money is a silver coinage in twenty cent denominations worth somewhat less than the more standard twenty cent coin. Actually, it is one of the many ways that the coolie and small shopkeeper has of confounding the foreigner, for no one, even many of those long here, are absolutely sure of its ratio to the more orthodox "big money" and always feel that they are being cheated out of something. And probably are.

This (the learned paragraph on finance)
gives us the opportunity to explain why
there is little chance for hostilities between
Japan and China. It seems that the whole
matter can be traced to the Japanese yen for
the Chinese tael. With these few remarks we
conclude our treatment of finance in the Far
East.

seen
on
the
streets

shops

THE TWO MOST commonly seen
commercial establishments on a Shanghai
street are the pawn shop and the medicine
shop. Both are always large and impressive
structures. The pawn shops always have a
large single character on the outside wall,
this character sometimes covering as much
as two hundred square feet and being two
stories high. Pawn shops are everywhere,
the reason being that the lower class Chinese
continuously keep some of their jewelry or
gems in hock. Instead of putting valuables

into pawn in times of financial duress, they reverse the procedure and take them out during periods of affluence. The reason for the redundance of the Chinese pawn shop can thus be seen. The cause for frequency of the Medicine Shop is probably brought about by the prevalence of disease of all kinds amongst the people. These shops are also large and ornate and often have some sort of a sculptured group above the doorway, in which the central figure is invariably a man with a long white beard. Inside, in the rather shadowy interior, are to be discerned casks, wood boxes and urns in large quantities. Animal remains and herbs from all over the world are brought to these places, ground, pulverized and otherwise prepared. Amazing prices are asked and paid for these potions. For instance, the pulverized tip of a deer's horn, used to prolong life, brings a hundred dollars a copy. Lately, hospital cars, painted white and fitted out as clinics by the Settlement and Frenchtown authorities, are giving serious competition to the medicine shops. They drop anchor anywhere in the street and dispense treatment and relief to the sick at little or no cost.

The Chinese have a tendancy to departmentalize their merchandising districts. For instance, on Foochow Road for several blocks above Hunnan Road, nothing is found but book and stationary stores, card printers and chop makers. At Canton Road below Hupien, there is a district of men's clothiers, further north on Hupien Road, a rash of men's tailors, on Kiukiang between Honan and Fokien practically nothing but jewelers and valuable Objets d'art (Chinese style — no appeal for foreigners) and probably most interesting to foreigners, there is, on Canton Road, for several blocks east of Kwangse, a colony of stores selling nothing but the wierd if colorful gowns, wigs, false beards, swords and other paraphanalia of the Chinese Theater.

Shanghai streets are to be heard (and smelt) as well as seen. A continual hubbub is a concommittant of the general scene, with riksha pullers constantly shouting their high-pitched warning to the slow-moving,

noisy conversations ever in progress, and
the calls of the foot peddlers. Every street
seems to have it's music, (or what passes for
music in China), whether it comes from the
thoroughly unmusical bands that Chinese
merchants hire to play from windows above
their stores to advertise sales or from the
shrill radio music coming from Chinese
broadcasting stations. Every type of street
merchant has an individual sound peculiar

29

to his business. Key grinders and knife sharpeners attach to their paraphanalia a collection of metal strips which jangle as the grinder walks. Sidewalk restaurant keepers bang away on a section of hollow bamboo. Sellers of musical instruments perform

upon their own instruments as they walk along and other peddlers of various kinds evolve noise from everything from gongs to whistles.

One of the commonest type of business place is the small-time bank, or "change shop." These are small establishments, one or more to the block, which lend small sums to local merchants upon personal guarantee, no collateral necessary. They also do a business in changing money, charging three coppers for the transaction. Behind the barred counters of these establishments, the money changer and what is apparently the total male complement of his family can be seen, lounging in bored opulance. Cigarette shops in China also sell joss sticks, paper taels (to he burned in the temples) and various other accoutrements of the religion rackett.

Provision stores are frequent and odorous. Butcher shops may be picked out from the position of the butcher, who operates on his subjects from a throne high above the heads of the customers. This is apparently another piece of Chinese cunning intended to outsmart people who say "Why, that's all bone!" Rice stores sell rice and other cereals alone, dipping them out in scoopfuls from bins sunk in the counters. On Foochow Road, there is a particularly attractive shop specializing in the sale of duck gizzards, with hundreds — thousands of duck gizzards hanging in the windows, from the ceilings, to the walls. Nice thought.

One of the things most striking to foreigners is the apparent over supply of employees. Every shop has about three times the number of clerks that one would find in any other country, most of them apparently having little else to do than to look blank. The idea seems to be that anyone who has had the fortune to rise in the world to the position of owning a shop or other establishment is also on the spot insofar as his brothers, cousins, nephews and other relatives are concerned. He is rather obligated to give them some kind of employment whether he wants to or not. Which explains why so many Chinese are content to remain coolies.

The second hand clothing stores
are perhaps the noisiest types of store in
Shanghai. The salesmen stand in front of
the shops holding the clothing at arms
length and reciting their virtues in a high
pitched sing song voice. With two dozen
salesmen going into their act at the same
time, something resembling a cock-eyed
version of a Gregorian chant results, which is
something very choice in screwness.

Every block seems to have three or four
coolie restaurants. Cooking and eating takes
place in one big room entirely open to the
street on one side to permit the smoke and
fumes and customers to get out. The food is
about the same, day by day, and the baking
is done in a large earthenware jug. The fire
is in the bottom, the oven at the top, a hole
in the side and at the top providing the
draught. One of the cooks fans air into the
hole at the side to increase the oven heat.
Coolies love to eat and do so every time they
get a little money ahead, which accounts for
the prevalence of these restaurants. Ricksha
coolies drop off at some restaurant between

fares to spend a large portion of the last money earned upon a bowl of noodles or a freshly baked *f'vai wu*.

merchants on the move

STREET MERCHANTS ARE as common as Englishmen in London. Most of them don't seem to do much business but they apparently get a lot of exercize. There are those who sell peeled sugar-cane (ready for gnawing) and these are probably most common.

There are others who deal in watermelon seeds, sunflower seeds, peeled carrots, cakes, candies, shoe strings, ear cleaners, and all other commodities. There are sidewalk restauranteurs, who carry food, stove, dishes and all suspended from a bamboo pole over the shoulders and are able, at any time, to stop and give you a full course dinner, if you desire it, say on the corner of Nanking Road and the Bund.

There are traveling seamstresses who perch on your doorstep and takes the holes out of your socks and shoemakers whose shoulder borne load includes all the leather and tools necessary to repair or even make a pair of shoes for you.

other sidewalk phenonena

EVEN IN THE coldest weather, sidewalk business is popular in Shanghai. This is probably because the Chinese will stop to watch anything. If one bends over to fix a shoe lace, he will straighten up to find himself the center of a staring crowd.

Street altercations gather mobs. A traffic mix-up interests everyone but the police who nonchalantly show up only after all participants exhaust their capacity for abuse.

The Sihk policeman is perhaps one of the most interesting spectacles of the Shanghai streets. Tall and impressive, turbaned and bearded, they carry out their duties with irrefutable authority and yet with a philosophically humorous understanding

of what its all about. A Chinese policeman
in violant argument with a coolie who has
violated a street ordinance. Suddenly a Sihk
policemen approaches, indomitably, like the
Juggernaut down Calcutta's streets, his white
teeth flashing in an amused smile, grasps the
coolie firmly by the ear, leads him out of the
laughing crowd to a spot further down the
street, where a well-directed motion of the
boot puts an end to the situation.

Coolies sharing heavy burdens add to
the general street din with their cries of
Ho–Ha–Ho, each taking his turn in
alternating the cry. An occasional wedding
or funeral adds a little color to the general
scene.

With rickshas coming and going in every
direction, and following no set procedure in
traffic, and people, after the Chinese fashion,
walking in the streets more often than on the
sidewalks, which are apparently for the use
of small vendors and merchants, a Chinese
street scene is one of chaos and turmoil.

Ricshas are of two varieties, private and
public. The public ones bear two license

plates, one with their license number
and another bearing a scale of rates. The
public ricksha is somewhat higher and less
comfortable and is certainly plenty more
dirty while the private ricksha is usually
lower, much more carefully painted and
polished and in the winter is equipped
with a lap robe. Private families of means
sometimes have very ornate rickshas
with copper plated running boards, fancy
upholstery, and as the greatest novelty of

all, clean pullers. Ricsha coolies are perhaps the most conscientious chiselers on earth. Worldly and quick to capitalize on any situation, they will, with bland face, make the most outrageous demands and moan all over the place if their demands are not satisfied.

The Chinese bargain in advance with them. Picture of a Chinese woman engaging a ricksha. She makes known her destination, looking the other way as if she were not greatly interested in going to that spot, and might change her mind if the price were not right. Coolie sets a price that he knows he doesn't stand a chance of getting. Woman commences to loftily walk away. Coolie follows loudly citing reasons why his ricsha is the best ricsha in China. Woman ignores him commencing to call (not very loudly) for another ricsha. Coolie comes down in his price muttering meanwhile about lady's stinginess. Lady still doesn't know he's there. About the time that all the other ricshas within ten blocks are charging up at the top of their lungs, coolie is down to his rock-bottom price and the lady climbs into the seat with studied magnificence. Fadeout, lady and ricsha coolie happily tooling along towards the horizon.

Sidewalk stands are frequent. Outside of the usual purveyors of foods, sweets, sugar-cane and small personal articles, there are upon the pavements representatives of the arts. Letter writers are common, each behind his table and willing to offer his services to the first illiterate who comes along wanting to write to his cousin in Soochow. Somewhat similar in appearance are the fortune tellers who will permit those curious about the future to choose a rolled up scroll from a number of these in a box, and interpret that scroll for them in terms of astrology, psycho-analysis or what have you.

An interesting street-sight to the newcomer is sometimes found on Bubbling Well Road at Mohawk Road. There, fronting the stables are two stone gods that are regarded by stable boys and Chinese riders as being "good joss" and one often sees in passing quantities of latzoh or punk sticks burning, placed there by devotees to both gods and horses in the hope that their particular nag will nose in first. Amahs with "sidewalk girls" in tow do the same thing as a prelude to the night's work.

Booksellers are also plentiful displaying numbers of books against somebody else's wall, most of them being volumes popular with the grandfathers and great grand-fathers of the people who shuffle by in front of them. Dealers in art plaster the walls with lurid lithographs of girls reclining (rather uncomfortably it seems to Western eyes though most of them seem to be smiling bravely), girls in aviator's helmets, girls about to take a bath, apparently, and just girls.

Foreigners sometimes wonder at the sight of a Chinese with what are apparently circular black pieces of court plaster on either side of the eyes on the lower temple. Those, ladies and gentlemen, are the China-side substitute for lisperin. Those are headache eradicators. Another curiosity is the outer clothing of young infants which is always a

brilliant scarlet. Still another common sight
are the mourning shoes of the male, white
and very similar to the footwear in which the
un-Chinese play tennis.

A common sight is a person in the throes
of some sort of fit, badly hurt or ill lying
on the pavement with a circle of apathetic
persons about him. Such a person will never
be assisted by anyone in the crowd that
gathers around him or her for it is a Chinese
belief that to do so renders one responsible
for that person from then on and for his soul
in case he dies.

The Chinese street scene is a colorful
one, diverse, swift moving and capable of
producing any kind of a situation. Hoarse
shouts and shrill cries, staccato sounds from
bamboo section drums, the wail of native
violin or flute, the blare of an unbelievably
lousy advertising band and the constant
monotonous obligatto of human voices.
People of almost every type, in every stage of
opulance or poverty, health or wretchedness,
race, color and breed. Beggers, monks in
flowing black robes, coolies grunting under

loads that a union stevedore would split
into three, sihks stalking proudly through
the Chinese in overcoats usually three
sizes two small for them and followed
by their women in grotesque but colorful
flowing robes, modern Chinese in Kollege
Kut Klothing who avoid the mud puddles
very carefully and give a cold stare to their
gowned countrymen, carefully primped
girls strutting along as disdainfully as if it
were a worldful of coolies, old-regime ladies
tottering uncomfortably along on bound
feet, baffled female American tourists from
Dunkett's Falls, Iowa, who are SIMPLY NOT
going to eat anything or drink any water
until they get back to the hotel, clutching
their guide-books, kodaks and sometimes
their noses, Japanese women in colorful
kimonas and obis teetering along on wooden
slippers and thinking, every time they are
jostled by a Chinese, "Well, it won't be long
now......" People—all kinds, the color and
tang and spice of China is not in it's temples
nor in it's lotus strewn gardens but in its
crowded streets.

nymphs de pave

NO SMALL PART of the noctural street scene in Shanghai is contributed by the ladies whose commodity is love, cash and carry.

Thibet Road between Avenue Eddie the Seventh and Nanking Road is practically infested with these charming ladies from the earliest sign of twilight until three and four in the morning. From one A.M. on, the region around Kiukiang Road and on over to Peking Road from Nanking Road is the hunting ground of the damsels and hunting ground it is. The weak of resistance are the prey of sometimes two and three of the gals who work in a concerted onslaught, grasping the victim firmly by the clothing and doing their best to work him into a doorway or other place where they can compromise him to the extent that he loses face if he doesn't accede.

Each girl is accompanied by an amah, who recites her protege's charms, virtues and accomplishments and otherwise negotiates with the clients. Meanwhile, the girl stands by and looks bored.

On a warm evening hundreds of these girls are out, filling the street, giggling and wise-cracking at the appearance or demeanor of the male passers-by, horse-playing with each other like high school children while amah keeps a wary eye for customers and police. Sometimes the law puts in an appearance. Then all of the girls, like some startled colony of pygmies at the approach of giant. take to their heels in a wild rush for doorways and basements and the midnight street is left to the sardonically smiling ricsha coolies, who smile because they know that the only advantage they have that their trade is not unlawful

the
fleshpots

night life in shanghai

AS HAS BEEN said, night life in Shanghai owes much of its spontaniety and natural atmosphere to the fact that it is as much the year-in-and-out residents as the visitors who do the reveling at the town's night spots. People who never go for anything worse than a sundae at Schmidt's Sugar Bowl of a Saturday evening at home in Keokuk, regard themselves as stay-at-homes in Shanghai if they don't step out a couple of times a week.

The Chinese are also inveterate whoopee-makers. They love to get out and around and be seen at the smart places. However, excepting at the Chinese cabarets, they are received with not exactly the utmost in cordiality, in view of the fact that they practically never go in for hard liquor in a big way, sometimes spending an entire evening nursing a glass of tea. This sort of business, of course, gives the cash register no exercise. The Chinese pay their chits when presented, however, which is something.

Naturally, there are many phases to the night life of the town, many ways for many kinds of people.

If the general atmosphere of Shanghai seems to have a somewhat carmine hue, think nothing of it. So continuously and continually is the job of "painting the town red" done, that it's bound to show somehow.

Technically, there are but three ways of making whoopee in Shanghai. Number one is by sending the boy out for three quarts and some ice, and telephoning Clara and Dick to come over and lift a few. This is known as "going to town while remaining at home," and is the least expensive. Then there's the business of gathering the clan and making the spots, St. Georges, Del Montes, etc. and is known is some quarters as "going to the dogs." Can be expensive. And last, there are those who incase themselves in silk and white linen and sally forth to places of the cover charge type, the only real difference between this and the last class being that it takes them longer and more money to feel their liquor. This is known, (by the people in the second class) as "going highbrow" and can be extremely expensive

financially, coming under the heading of "major appropriations."

As a night life town, Shanghai is different from New York and other cosmopolitan centers in that it is the natives as well as the visitors who do the night revelling. Although at the time of the writing of this book, night entertainment business has been poor in Shanghai, the town's residents have supported their night clubs quite strongly.

Amongst the leading spots are the

Tower, atop the very gilt-edge Cathay
Hotel, the Sky Terrace, atop the Park Hotel,
the Paramount Ballroom and the Cathay's
ballroom which is purely a smart place to
dine and dance but doesnt remain open late.
The Little Club, long the most famous of
Shanghai's smart night clubs recently folded
up rather ingloriously after an attempt to
operate on somewhat different lines than
employed during its hey-day.

The Tower, under the able management
of the ambilinguistic Freddy Kaufmann
is one of the most popular spots. Singer,
pianist, intimate atmosphere, and so forth.
The Sky Terrace is notable principally for
the fine view of the racecourse and of the
electrically sensational Shanghai horrizon.
In other ways, it is exactly the sort of a
night spot one might find in Paris London
or New York. Good entertainment, genteel
surroundings. The Paramount is unique in
being one of the largest class good time spots
in town and offers a very deluxe product in
the way of entertainment, atmosphere, and
so on.

49

dime a dance, china style

THE CHINESE LOVE to dance. And do it very well. Surprisingly strange in a people whose national music sounds like tormented tom cats, is a sense of rythm that makes them excellent dancers, both men and women. And so, the cabaret business, distinct from the cafe and night club business, flourishes. And especially, Chinese cabarets, which are institutions quite unique.

The typical Chinese cabaret, large and spacious, it is usually decorated to the most remote corner, with perhaps a half a dozen incongruous and clashing types and styles of Western ornamentation fighting for honors. The orchestra, invariably Filipino, pumping away at a-tune-a-minute rate continuously between the hours of eight and two, three or four o'clock, rather lackadaisically esconced on the bandstand. Whitecoated table-boys by the score, about twice as many as necessary, since they work only for their tips and chow. The guests, mostly male,

very blase, apparently quite unaware of the dancings girls, or "*woo niuhs*" who sit but an arms-length away from them, noisily eating watermelon seeds, a dish of which are placed on each table by the management as a gratuitous gift. And last but most important, the *woo niuhs*, slim, nonchalant and self-possessed and self-sufficient to the nth degree, cuddling their miniature hot water bottles if it is winter time, and acting for all the world as if they were really just waiting for a street car and no amount of dance tickets could tempt them onto the floor.

The proper and recognized procedure seems to call for extremely snooty behavior on the part of the dancing girl until some stage of intimacy is reached. This means after about the tenth dance and is intended to give the general idea that she has plenty of business and didn't really need you at all. Girls in the better class dance places will not accept less than three or four dance tickets, and if offered a smaller amount will tear them up in the face of the giver. The idea is that if a client dances but once or so and passes on, the girl's charm, dancing ability or something is impuned. She lose "face" with her colleagues and contrives to pass some of that loss of face on to the guest in the above mentioned fashion.

Dancing girls are notoriously temperamental and their relations with the management are much the same as those between a prima donna and an opera

impressario. Arguments over trea
fancied slights and such trifles as t
of their chairs, etc are always arising and
popular girls have to be handled with
extreme unction as they will quit on the drop
of a watermelon seed.

The *woo niuhs* sit on the edge of the
ballroom floor in seats the arms of which
has been bored to hold a glass, kept filled
with tea. Service to the dancing ladies also
includes a boy (in the winter time) who is
kept busy keeping the hot water bottles of
the *woo niuh* filled.

The price of dance tickets varies from
three for a dollar at the best places to eight,
ten and even fifteen at some of the dives. The
girls receive on an average, about one half
of the price paid for the ticket, and some of
them, with gifts from their customers make
what is an enormous salary for China and for
a women. Two very popular sisters dancing
at one of the town's best spots are credited
with making a monthly salary of better than
a twelve hundred Shanghai dollars between
them.

The morals of the class are about the same as respectable women everywhere, that is adamantly negative most of the time, charmingly complaisant upon occasion. One outstanding feature of dancing girl character, however, is the complete dignity and composure displayed at all times even among the charmers in the worst Hongkew dives, and the absence of all vulgarity or coarseness from their conduct. No matter which of the many rather gaudy sins available in Shanghai a *woo niuh* chooses

to commit, you can be sure she will do it
gracefully, with dignity, her head in the air.

There are also many Russian, Japanese
and Korean dancing girls in Shanghai.
Strangely, there are no American, British
or other foreign hostesses. Places having
such varied groups to choose from proudly
advertise their "International Hostesses"
and invariably draw a heavy business from
young Chinese males.

some night spots...

HEADING THE BETTER Chinese cabarets
in Shanghai are the Majestic on Bubbling
Well Road across from the race course, the
Ambassador on Avenue Edward VII, the
Casanova (all Russian hostesses) on the same
street, with the well known Tom King at
the helm, Santa Anna's, on Love Lane, and
the two popular Bubbling Well resorts, the
Vienna Gardens and the Metropole Gardens.
The latter we believe, would give anyone
interested in the subject, the best possible

birds-eye view of what a high class Chinese cabaret is like.

Operated by "Jimmy," who keeps the restaurant mentioned elsewhere in these pages, is the St. Georges Cabaret on the Route Doumer in the French Concession. Though the premises of this cabaret are decidedly archaic and unattractive, the attendance is quite large.

Del Monte's, one of the latest closing spots in Shanghai is quite famous. It has quite an assortment of Russian, Hungarian and other assorted varieties of dancing girl, all of whom "double in bass", that is, dance for the customers individually as units in a floor show as well as dancing girl, with them for tickets. Known for years as a place to go when all of the other places had closed, Del Monte's is visited by all classes and types of people. It's most noteworthy distinction, perhaps, is a modified form of the old time honky-tonk atmosphere which persists despite the fact that the bouncers and other officials of the place have been buttoned into soup and fish outfits.

anything can happen at the venus

POSSIBLY THE BEST known and most colorful spot in Shanghai is the Venus Cafe. Located just inside of Chinese territory in Hongkew it is not subject to the early closing laws prevalent in the Settlement and opens its doors to nocturnal strays until the cold gray dawn filters down from the filthy rooftops abutting Jukong Alley. Owned by an agressive American named Levy, it has since it's existence attracted specimens from every stratum of Shanghai night life so that its purlieus resemble, on any night, the office of a movie casting director about to make a picture on the Far East.

A trip to the Venus is worth the sleep lost and is part of anyone's education. Getting out of your taxi at the juncture of North Szechuan Road and Jukong Alley, you are faced with the problem of getting to the garishly lit doors of the Venus without being blackmailed into contributing to the weal of some dozen beggers who apparently

base their importunities upon the fact that
as you are headed for a good time, common
decency demands that you supply their
demands. Chief amongst these gentry is a
tall cadaverous Russian youth with a meager
coat, collar up, clutched together with a
palsied hand. A white face, staring eyes
with a wordless appeal and mute, pinched
lips complete the act. This lad had us in a
state of incipient meloncholia for months

until we saw him, during Russian Easter, in very changed raiment, toddling a beauteous blonde into a sukiyaki parlor on the Avenue Joffre.

The first thing encountered upon entering the entrance of the Venus is a sign which reads "No More Chits Accepted." Then another succinct memorandum "Out of Bounds To British Troops." (The whole Hongkew area is out of bounds to American Troops). However it is distinctly "in bounds" to Japanese troops.

The cafe itself is not extraordinary in appearance. The usual conglommeration of artistic effects, the garish lighting effects (China is probobly the only place in the world where Neon lighting is used for interior illumination), and the routine force of dancing girls. The dancing girls at the Venus perhaps deserve a little more than the ordinary treatment in this volume. In the first place, these lasses are entirely in sympathy with the slogan of a large American manufacturer of paint "Save The Surface And You Save All." Some of them bear startling

resemblences to the Benda masks so popular
a few years ago while others, more subdued,
just look as if they had used the lipstick in
the wrong places. Dresses here are of the
going-to-town variety where decolletage
is concerned. More than half of the girls at
the Venus are Japanese. There are a number
of Chinese, Korean and a few Russian girls
but the Japanese gals seem to do all of the
business.

Entirely more interesting than the employees of the place, are the patrons. Sailors
on the lurch, brokers and proper business
men hoping that their number ones aren't
likely to hear of the trip to the Venus, their
number ones hoping that none of the employees see them, dinner coated parties slum-
ming and raggedy-rear parties high-lifing,
newspapermen, musicians, butchers, bakers
and sometimes a candlestickmaker or so.

The Venus begins to come to life at about
three when some of the other spots begin
to close. Four kinds of people go there. The
people who don't go to Del Montes, the
people who want to sin conspicuously, the

people who want to sin inconspicuously and those who have that happy alcoholic feeling, and want to keep it. Musicians from the other night clubs show up for the same reason that busmen are said to go for a busride on the day off. The dancing girls make their boy-friends takes them there because it gives them an uppity feeling to relax and play before the working dancing girls in the place, and also to chat with their colleagues and discuss the day's business. Then, in addition to the high toned foreign visitors, there is the usual background of petty gangsters, dance hall play boys, American marines in civilian clothing, and assorted drunks. The Venus is popular with the Japanese too and girls in the Nipponese kimona and obi are quite a common sight, creating a somewhat refreshingly colorful contrast to the tawdry magnificence of the place.

From three until towards five, a carnival atmosphere abounds. Everyone gets nut and dances, excepting sometimes the formally clad ones from the drawing rooms, who stare glassily out upon the antics of Boatswain's Mate 3rd. Cl. Whitey Jones, who has forty dance tickets in his pocket and is going to town with Sizouki San in a great big way.

As the party begins to grow less hectic, as the prosaic yield to yawns and the ladies yield to importunities, the waiters are to be found sneaking off the unused table covers, the music becomes slightly less danceable, and the dancing girls who are not engaged frankly curl up in their chairs, wrap their coats about them, and abandoning their earlier graceful poses keep their date with

how to kill a lonely evening in shanghai

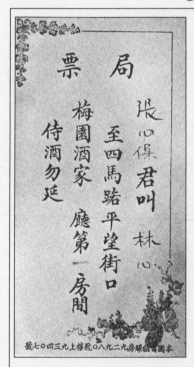

Request for a sing song girl

Mr. Chang Sing Pao requests that Miss Ling Shing come to the Mei Yuen Cafe, Room No. 1, address Ping Vong street, corner of Foochow Road to serve wine and entertain.

Do not delay.

Facsimile and illustration of Sing Song Girl request. Restaurants keep these forms on hand at all times, Male customers fill in the proper data, the chit is sent, and a lonely evening turned into something to write home about.

the sandman. Not permitted to go home
until the last note is played, they make the
best of it.

Outside in Jukong Alley, its cold and
gray and dismal. The beggers droop dismally
along the walls, ready to spring into whining
activity at the outward swing of the Venus
door. The fat old Russian wench fondles the
Shirley Temple photographs that are her
excuse for begging. The little alley which
a few hours before was picturesque and
atmospheric becomes sordid and ugly. Dawn
has checked in at the Venus.

the primrose path,
de luxe

MUCH HAS BEEN written about Sing Song
house. If one, however, cherishes romantic
illusions that these famed versions of the
mundaine seraglios of other lands are wildly
lurid rendezvous where one can give the
fleshpots an awful workout and help ones
self to an armful of beautiful Sin, amidst

scenes of Oriental volupte, one is distinctly
wrong.

Strangely enough, decorum, "good form"
and the observance of what to Westerners
is a very stiff and stilted ettiquette, are the
keynotes of the activities between the class a
ghee niu, or Sing Song girl, and her customer
or customers. In other words, raised
eyebrows and extreme coldness would be
accorded the would-be sinner who sailed
into one of the very elite establishments on
Swatow Road sailed his hat onto the rack,
slapped the amah on her posterior, and
greted the assembled *niuh* with a cosy "Hello
Toots". The procedure is somewhat different.

In the first place, a Sing Song house
is about the only establishment of its kind
that very emphatically discourages foreign
clients. Possibly because other Chinese
males, with the secret distaste felt by them
for sharing intimate occasions in Western
company, or perhaps because the egotism
of the sufficiency is distasteful to the
pathalogically sensitive egotism of the Sing
Song girl.

Painted generously, scented extravagantly and arrayed in attractive if rather extreme versions of the prevailing Chinese mode, the *ghee niu* is borne by her ricsha coolie to the scene of her professional activities, shortly after the shades of evening have fallen. Most of her engagements are made by appointment and she entertains her guests in various ways; by singing, by reciting, playing upon Chinese musical instruments or participating in card, finger or mah jong games. Finger games are very popular, possibly because they give onlookers a chance to vicariously enjoy the game, by kibitzing, wise-cracking and howling uproariously at every play. Two people play, each thrusting one hand out with any or all of the five fingers upraised. Alternately, each player calls out a number from one to ten with each thrust. If the total of fingers upraised from the hands of both players equals the number called, the person who has called the number wins the bet. Good clean fun, considering everything.

In Sing Song houses of the best class, the

customer and not the girl, is the wooer. In fact, the granting of her favors is entirely up to the *ghee niu* herself, and for a man to woo a lady for many moons and finally wind up with the air for his pains, is not unusual. In any case, many visits are required before any comparative degree of intimacy is attained. And of course, during these visits, much wine and tea is consumed, much food eaten, and many games of cards played (at twenty-four dollars a game to the house) so the management is not concerned as to the when or the if of the damsel's surrender.

Another departure from the conventional is the business method employed by such places, which is distinctly not on a cash and carry basis as elsewhere in the world. The display of money is considered decidedly vulgar. Statements for the services of the house and the *ghee niu* are sent to a customers office or home at regular intervals, and adjusted by the seraglio's regular shroff, or bill collector. Obligations of this sort are regarded by Chinese somewhat in the manner that Westerners regard gambling debts, as being debts of honor, requiring payment before all other matters. Gentlemen about to go bankrupt invariably settle their sing-song debts before declaring their insolvency. However, failure to pay does occur and sing song houses sue and collect, not only in Chinese courts but in the courts of the International Settlement, presided over by decorous foreigners who must gravely hand down decisions in favor of these high class bordellos.

No stigma, normal or social, attaches
to the Sing Song house habitue. In fact
some of the town's elitest big shots with
large domestic establishments of their own,
make these places their regular nocturnal
headquarters, and give parties in them
for their friends. One of the advantages
in this system, of course, is that if your
dinner partner bores you, you can make an
exchange.

Entertainment is not cheap. An evening's
dalliance will cost in the neighborhood of
sixty or seventy dollars Shanghai currency, at
a minimum, and can run as high as several
hundred dollars easily. The financial standing
of the clientele can be judged from the sight
each evening of lines of large, expensive cars
in this district, their chauffeurs lounging
in groups discussing, probably, the morals,
disposition, virility and amorous proclivities
of their dallying masters.

Most of the Sing Song girls are very
young, between the ages of fifteen and
twenty-one or two, although girls with

exceptional personality and physical attractiveness have worked at an older age. Unlike their Japanese colleagues of the same profession, there is no excess of gray matter hidden away beneath the jewelled black ringlets of the *nius*. The majority of them fall very easily into the category of beautiful and dumb.

Lovemaking between the Sing Song girls and their swains takes a very strange form. Not until the very final intimacies does any form of spoken endearment occur. The first part of the courtship is spent in an

exchange of bantering derision, and lavishly imaginative comments upon the capabilities and shortcomings of the other party.

There are, of course, different grades of establishments. In some of the less exclusive establishments, Western civilization and culture has exerted it's influence, with the result that the inmates are treated with less consideration and the clients expect more action in less time. Occidental efficiency and the speed-tip system will soon have these century old establishments on a modern basis, or something.

Chinese may, and do often attempt to refute the fact that the Sing Song institution is prostitution in it's most genteel form. They hope to give a virtuous, platonic and aesthetic tone to a custom that so many high in public and business life subscribe to. But the fact remains that all of the musicmaking, card-playing and other forms of bought flirtation are but the means to an end without which the entire affair would lose it's significance, and be looked upon as so much lost time and money.

jukong and blood alleys

TWO CHOICE SPOTS are Jukong Alley and Blood Alley, each at opposite extremes of the town, at either side of the Settlement.

Blood Alley, known to the genteel as the Rue Chao Pau San, is probably a sailor's idea of heaven. At night, this gentle area is a blaze of light, a blare of color and can he heard—almost felt—all the way down to the Bund. There are fifteen cabarets, starting with the Fantasio—very select—to the Ritz, which is also very nice, too. The street is filled with the animal life indigenous to such surroundings, taxi-hustlers, procurers, beggers, Russians willing-to-reveal-the-night-life, ricsha coolies, massage house steerers, stolid Annamite policemen and optimistic sharpshooters of every stripe and hue. Sailors, marines and occasional civilians of every nationality wander, teeter and finally stagger from place to place, pausing only now and then to punch each other on the nose as the occasion demands.

Apparently assault only becomes a violation of French law when bones are broken, or maybe nothing counts on Blood Alley as long as both parties keep their fingers crossed, because few people get arrested there.

Just the other side of the Settlement gate, and in the Chinese late-closing area, is Jukong Alley, scene of the Venus Cabaret, already described. Here are probably the greatest collection of honky-tonk cafes ever assembled on one street. Most of them are Russian, some are Japanese, all of them something extra special in what the Well Dressed Man is avoiding this season. That is, outside of the Venus, and an especially choice resort, called the Red Rose, quite popular with the Russians.

Here at the Red Rose, where Russian Gypsy music and singing gets a big play, they have an act which bids fair to be the best act in town. A woman (very enbonpoint) creaks out onto the floor to sing a painfully operatic number. In the midst of the number, a man can be perceived stealing out of the kitchen. He pauses behind a post, hurls a coin out onto the floor, and whips back into the kitchen. The coin is a decoy. People are supposed to follow suit and drown out the song with the music of falling silver. But no one ever does. Sometimes the stooge from the kitchen tries again. Nothing ever happens. One of life's minor tragedies but very fascinating after the fourth or fifth visit to the Red Rose. You get to waiting for the man to steal out of the kitchen.

there
are
also
some
chinese
in
shanghai

quaint people really

TO MOST FOREIGNERS there are but two
kinds of Chinese, the clean and the dirty.
However, the situation is more complex than
that. There are Chinese who like foreigners
and those who do not and are very much in
the majority. There are Chinese who are very,
very Western, modern and sophisticated
in their activities and outlook and other

Chinese who condemn them seriously
for being so. Then there are the "returned
students," so earnestly and garrulously
interested in the promotion of Occidental-
Oriental goodwill, with committees and
associations and other impedimenta, that

its rather painful. And of course, there are always the coolies who, if somewhat filthy and noisome, are at least without inhibitions or complexes.

The younger Chinese are split into two groups. One is an eutrasmart, very sports-clothsy, country-clubular set with all of the nuances of Long Island and Mayfair behaviorism, which is something that Freud really missed. The other group, in greater majority, are seriously following a back-to-China movement, which means a reversion from the foreign influence of the past thirty years and a return to real Chinese, customs, dress, manners, philosophy, intellectualism and conduct of life. Which gives them the edge on the ultra moderns.

In any case, the better class Chinese of both camps go in for social life in a great big plentiful way. Teas, balls, dances, garden parties and benefits till it hurts. And Chinese women are assisted in their adoration of the social amenities by the fact that male Chinese don't mind getting into the soup-and-fish — in fact they like to — and the result is that even the most ordinary of Chinese acairs are good copy for the rotogravure section. In the past, parties of mixed foreigners and Chinese were quite common, but there has been a tendency toward the inclusion of less foreign guests more recently. Possibly the failure of Western nations to intercede in Far Eastern crises the way they did in bygone times may have something to do with the not-so-amiable attitude of the Chinese.

It is considered quite a personal compliment for a foreigner to be invited to a Chinese home for what is known colloquially a "Chinese Chow." We will not go into detail here upon the details of a Chinese dinner, having dealt with it elsewhere in this learned treatise, but we will just mention that it is rather incongruous to come to such a party, sip a cocktail with the assembled guests in Western style and be considerably impressed with the cultured English, informed conversation and evidences of what Occidentals regard as breeding displayed by all hands, and then go into the dining room, and see said persons eating from communal

dishes in the center of table, with lavish
contributions to the table cloth, sucking
in edible fluids with complete abandon,
ejecting from their mouths the undesirable,
and getting as close to the foodstuffs during
the entire performance as their noses will
let them. Or maybe its the fault of the
chopsticks.

Chinese women are quite lovely and
exotic in appearance. Their long, panel

gowns fitted to their generally slim bodies, their coifure perpetually perfect in its delightful complication, and invariably small feet in possibly smaller shoes, they unquestionably score insofar as appearance is concerned. For some reason, foreign women are completely unable to wear Chinese clothing with anything approaching

the effect achieved by the Chinese, in fact they look pretty terrible in them for the reason that the Occidental curves are in different places, if you follow us. And if you do, you shouldn't. And while on the subject of Chinese women, we want to go on record as exposing the age-old Occidental belief concerning their physiognomy. In the words of a certain United States senator, after his first twenty-four hours in Shanghai, "It aint so!"

Chinese men are of no interest to anyone except themselves. They wear long black gowns, like tea and grow rather obese after forty.

The lower classes, always safe to discuss, offer many and diverse opportunities for comment of various sorts. Males of the working classes can be roughly if vaguely divided into two classes, coolies and boys. We have never been exactly certain as to how to definitely differentiate between certain products of these two classes that seem to merge, but we can best advise you that a "boy", technically speaking, seems to be a washed coolie. Also the word "Boy" spoken in a loud voice, denotes that you want something done that in the United States, you would do yourself. Houseboys, or domestic servants as you will be surprised to learn, are a class to themselves, almost a race to themselves. They know more about you than you know yourself, and think less. They infest the dark regions under the stairs and back of the kitchen and are always going to send out the laundry tomorrow when you expected it back today.

houseboys, and other necessary evils

WHEN A HOUSEHOY gets to the point that he knows about all of the discreditable things about his master and missy, he is made a "number one boy." One of the best qualifications for the post of number one boy is a competance at getting rid of shroffs, or bill collectors. This, coupled with an ability to tactfully awaken and dispose of mislaid inebriates from the night before, before master and missy come down to breakfast, constitutes the repertoire of a perfect number one boy.

Much is said of the efficiency of Number One Boys. In fact, even the least vain of men are apt to boast about their boys, and will recite long boring stories to prove their boy's ability, resourcefulness and intelligence.

And so we tell the story of the Number One Boy whose master was very proud of him. Master went state-side to marry his childhood sweetheart, did so, and came back to China. All the way back, he talked his bride silly with yarns about the number one boy. Finally, after some delay and difficulty on the last lap of their trip, they arrived late at night at the young master's home, and turned in.

Next morning, the young busband arose and left for the office leaving his wife to sleep. The number one boy came in, took a look at the situation, went out, and returned with a five dollar bill which he tucked into the sleeping wife. She awoke with a start.

"Can go now, Missy" said the omiscient
number one. "Masta have gone work."

Chinese life is essentially elemental,
being hampered with nothing more complex
than the ageold superstitions which are
fighting a losing battle with the apathy
toward such things that civilization brings.
Still the old custom persist.

Chief amongst the current observances
of old custom are the funeral and the
marriage rites, and even these are gradually
under-going a blending with Western

custom. Many Chinese girls of ordinary class marry in veil and after Western fashion.

delicacies, delicate and otherwise

CHOP SUEY AND chow mein, the standard Chinese dishes in New York, San Francisco or Oshkosh, are practically unknown in China. These are American dishes with a dash of the Chinese to appeal to the American taste for the different.

Eating in China is still a fine art, and the one activity in life that the Chinese are serious about. They may laugh and joke at their funerals and weddings, but eating is a ritual. Much time and patience is required for the eating as well as the cooking of a meal which varies from four to fifty courses with the variability of the host's pocket book.

Tea is the oldest of Chinese customs, and means to "break the fast," for by serving the tea one "breaks the silence." In fact Chinese drink their tea from very early morning until late at night. Without sugar, cream, or lemon, it is always served immediately upon arrival at a Chinese dinner, showing that the visitor is welcome. A wise old Chinese poet said, "The first cup of tea moistens my lips and throat. The second cup breaks my loneliness . . . . The fourth cup raises a slight perspiration, all wrong passed away. The fifth cup I am purified, and the sixth cup I am called to the realm of the immortals." After the sixth cup, one is about ready for the immortals.

Tea is followed by the serving of hot towels, which are not used as napkins, but to "refresh one's self" and often quite frankly as wash cloths, the custom having originated in the northern part of China where it is extremely dusty. Incidentally, hot towels are passed to patrons in Chinese theaters also, which is an excellent idea, and couldn't be overdone.

As to food, sharks' fin is a great delicacy. It is the culinary name for the rows of cartileges inside each fin of a shark. It takes a long and tedious process of treatment and

boiling, but the result is tender
(if you like them). They are then
in their original symmetrical for
variety, they are served with potted chicken
sauce, shredded chicken, boiled chicken, in
egg omelet, and also served neat with brown
sauce.

Birds Nest soup, made from a gelatinous
substance found in the nests of swallows on
the rocky and precipitous coastal regions
of Indo China and the South Sea Islands, is
considered very nutritious. Because of this
fact, and its rarity, it is often the principal
dish in a meal, served either as clear soup
with diced or potted chicken or with pigeon
eggs. A Chinese dinner usually has two or
more soups served in between the other
courses.

Chicken in some form is the most
popular food. Every Chinese restaurant and
provision store has its rows of half-cooked
chickens hanging perpetually in the window.
The most tender and finest chickens are
imported into Shanghai from Canton, where
they are fed special food and raised in an

environment as select as the finest finishing school. They are easily distinguishable from the Shanghai chickens by the smallness of their feet, which are served with the meat, as a mark of authenticity. Among the chicken dishes we especially recommend are barbecued chicken, sliced chicken with bamboo shoots, shredded chicken rolls and diced chicken with almonds or walnuts. We also recommend the boneless sweet and sour pork, and the spring rolls.

A suggested menu is given and we hope that you live thru it. Roast duck, cold ham, spiced chicken, sweet pickles, fried shrimp balls, chicken fillet with bamboo shoots, sliced whelk meat with liver, "Gold Coin" chicken, sharks finns with brown sauce, stuffed quail, fried Kwangse turtle in soup, barbecued duck with ham, birds nest soup with pigeon eggs, barbecued Canton chicken, spring rolls with pork, vegetarian's dish de luxe, boneless sweet and sour pork, steamed fish with clear sauce. For dessert, noodles and sweet date soup. This menu is no longer than the Chinese eat every day by their social

dinners, but then it has been said that one fourth of their food goes to nourish them and three fourths to kill them. It probably also accounts for the prevalence of ailments among the wealthy or the political class, and it serves as an excellent excuse to retire when the going gets a bit rough.

oriental wassail

NO CHINESE MEAL is complete without wines, which may be divided into three groups. The wines of the north are usually very strong, and somewhat like vodka in flavor. The Shao Hsing (pronounced "Shoshing") wine of the Yangtze Delta region is somewhat like sherry in its strength and flavor and is the most papular. It is the wine used in place of champagne for official ceremonies, such as the christening of a ship or plane. It is always served warm and has an exquisite mellow flavor agreeable to most foreigners. The Cantonese wines are of various strengths and mild and sweet as to flavor. All Chinese wines are served from pots.

After months and months (or is it years) our imagination is not up to really describing coolie chow vividly enough so that you may get a true picture, which is probably just as well. In the first place, it is sold by street hawkers, in open stalls and from door to door. The most popular coolie dish is noodles, served either plain or with meat, the price of the bowl of noodles varying with the number of pieces of meat, as each additional piece adds to the cost. Second day noodles are considered a greater delicacy than first day noodles. They have been allowed to cool and sour just enough to appeal to the Chinese taste. *F'vei wu* ranks second only to the noodles, in the heart of a coolie, and is also sold by all street vendors. It is made in some mysterious fashion from beef, peeled, chopped very fine, mixed with fat, and so highly seasoned with soya sauce that it is almost black. It is then molded into an enormous mellon-shaped cake, which keeps for several days. When an individual portion of "*fvei wu*" is wanted, it is scooped out from the underneath side of the mold, mixed with rice, and put inside a ball of dough, and heated. It is one of the great out-door sports of the town (so far as coolies are concerned) to argue as to the amount of meat that goes into the ball. You might take one of these home and try it on some of your in-laws. We didn't go for it.

The Cantonese apparently have more intestinal fortitude in the matter of food than the Northerners, for they eat many things that are not eaten in or about Shanghai. To be offered a snake is a rare treat and great honor. The snakes are carefully raised and fed special food. They are cleaned in the same manner as fish, slit up the midle and put on the table whole, where it is then sliced. The meat is firm, white and inclined to be very oily.

A ceremonial dish, served at banquets and formal dinners is *what t'sen* which is a steak taken from a monkey.

Field mice, skinned and fried in deep fat, is a very popular dish among the coolie class in this part of the country. At one time the eating of cats was a common custom, but Western influence has partially done away with this, as far as we know. During great famines they have been known, though rarely, to resort to eating babies, but as they so naively put it, "they don't eat them as rare as the British eat their beef". . . . Oh Well!

Talking of food probably ranks second only to the eating of it, and the eating certainly ranks first in the heart of any good Chinese (or bad).

(滬大) 士女三英鳳顧雲美周君鳳顧

Misses F. C. KOO, M. Y. CHOW and F. Y. KOO

the beggar kingdom

OUTSIDE OF RETURNED students and business men, the best English spoken in Shanghai by Chinese, is spoken by the begger class. Please understand that these are not ordinary beggers, requiring from the world, in exchange for a plaintive whine, a pittance that will sustain a wretched existence. These high toned mendicants are professionals, masters of their art, specialists in whatever form of argonizing that their art may take.

The beggers guild, an organization that has put begging on a paying basis in Shanghai, is better and more effectively organized than the Standard Oil Company. A prospective member is examined as to his capabilities and rated accordingly. If he has always been a whining begger and the guild comes to the conclusion that his capabilities are of a different hue and he's been wasting his time whining for people when the market is already glutted with whiners, then he is persuaded to change his act. Ragged suits

(often very patently ragged) are provided.
He or she is encouraged to get good and
dirty (excessive coaxing is not necessary) and
then with the character created, the scene
is laid. Shanghai is plotted out by the guild
and beggers are allocated to certain beats
with systematic finesse. And their locale is
changed carefuly from time to time. In this
way, though there are thousands of beggers,
one never sees mobs of them together, as in
India, and, on the other hand, no important
spot is without it's outstretched palm, or
palms. Their rights are carefully protected by
the guild and in many other ways they are
taken care of. For all of this benevolence, the
beggers from their not-too-bad earnings, pay
a regular cut to the guild.

Nauseously afflicted and eyeless,
maimed or otherwise repulsive mendicants
are as common as Englishmen with
adenoids. Female beggeresses carrying
enormous children well able to walk abound.

Many of the mendicants are good
entertainers. Jugglers (after a fashion),
are common. Along the wharves, begging

acrobats do very well, especially when cruise ships, packed with tourists, are in. There are also singing beggers (usually women and very poor singers, even for Chinese style) and comic beggers, whose comedy consist for the main part, of grimaces and the effect of grotesque hats.

Most interesting to foreigners are the small girl and boys who beg in the foreigner-infested district about the Cathay Hotel and Bund region. The stock-in-trade of these children, who are between the ages of five and fifteen, is an immense geniality, a keen knowledge of what will make the foreigners laugh, a remarkable gift for repartee, and all the personality in the world.

The little girl who makes her plea for money on the basis that she has "no mama, no papa, no home, no chow, no whiskey-soda" is famous. This damsel knows her customers, spots them a long way off, and will follow a ricksha for blocks, making the most personal remarks and enquiries, until her victim pays off. Quite definitely interested in the affairs and activities of her clients, she will, if she sees someone that she knows in the company of a women with whom she has never seen the man before, shout out "Whatsa matter, mastah, have got new missy? Where old missy go?"

Foreigners are good customers, usually because they are amused or rendered sympathetic by the stories told. The Chinese are good givers but for a different reason, feeling that it gives them face to give to a begger. Chinese prostitutes, dancing and Sing Song girls are legitimate prey for the mendicant class, as they are generous givers. Unfortunately for the face of foreigners amongst the Chinese, Russian beggers are comparitively common and are not above soliciting alms from the Chinese themselves.

and in conclusion

WITH THIS SYMPATHETIC critique of the profession which seems happier and more prosperous than any other group in town, Chinese or foreign, we wind up our interpretation of the multi-colored and complex

Bagdad-on-the Whangpoo known as Shanghai.

One more thing before closing—
something that might be termed "the
Shanghai ilusion." Many otherwise
intelligent people, misled by gaudy fiction
on the East and by wacky movies produced
by directors whose ideas of China were
garnered in midwestern chop suey joints,
conceive it to be an eerie place peopled with
sinister Orientals, embittered remittance men
slowly going to hell, gin sling in hand, and
painted adventuresses casting spells whilst
murmuring cynical epigrams (Marlene
Deitrich-like). Well, women paint and cast
spells in Shanghai (just as they do in Snyder's
Falls, Vermont) and men drink and go to
hell (and return) and it's rumored about that
there are a few Chinese in the town. But
as the incipiently-disapponted believers in
such yarns find out, all of this is but part of
"the Shanghai illusion" and is as phoney as a
Hollywood opium joint.

Shanghai is a grand town. Not an
atmospheric background for Oriental
melodrama, but a grand place to live, to

work and to enjoy life.

Many profess to hate the town, and to be waiting eagerly for a chance to depart. Chances come and go and yet they seem to linger on, making excuses for their dalliance.

And when they do go, those who have spent some time here and come to know the place, there comes a feeling of regret as they sail down the river looking back at the Bund for the last time, a feeling that wherever they are going they will always want to come back.

The old town must have something.

Other Books
in the Earnshaw Books
China Classics
Series

See
www.TalesOfOldChina.com/store
for details